ENVISION
ENLIGHTEN
ENRICH

ENVISION ENLIGHTEN ENRICH

RETIREMENT STRATEGIES FOR PROSPERITY AND PURPOSE

JIM ELIOS

Jim Elios
jim@eliosfinancial.com
www.EliosFinancial.com

Envision - Enlighten - Enrich, Jim Elios—1st ed.

CERTIFIED

(H)

WRITTEN
BY HUMAN

DEDICATION

This book is dedicated to my Mom and Dad, Thomas and Olympia Elios (Eliopoulos), who bravely left their families in Greece to pursue their version of the American Dream in the late 1950s. Your courage, determination, and sacrifices have inspired me every step of the way. This book is a tribute to your legacy and a reflection of the values you instilled in me.

To my wife Solveig, whose constant encouragement and unwavering belief in abundance have been my guiding light. Your love and support have made all things possible.

And to my three wonderful kids, James, Sophia, and Christina, who are an unending source of love and inspiration. Your joy, laughter, and curiosity remind me of life's true blessings every single day.

With heartfelt gratitude and love,

JTE

CONTENTS

Introduction *9*

1. Do You Have Everything You Need To Retire? How Will You Know? 11
2. Strong Principles Lead To Solid Retirement Planning 23
3. Successful Investing Is Directly Related To Your Behavior 33
4. Focus On What You Can Control For A Long, Happy Retirement 45
5. Don't Make Short-Term Decisions On Long-Term Money - Don't Make Long-Term Decisions on Short-Term Money 53
6. How Saving On Taxes Increases Long-Term Wealth 59
7. Two More Keys To Long-Term Wealth: Diversification And Low Fees 71
8. Wealth That Is Truly Priceless: Your Good Health 81
9. How To Move Your Retirement Forward With A Financial Advisor 89
10. Your Summary on Managing Financial Risk So You Can Enjoy Your Retirement 99

Conclusion *109*
About the Author *113*

INTRODUCTION

When I think about retirement, this quote from Patrick Foley says it all:

> "Retirement is a blank sheet of paper. It is a chance to redesign your life into something new and different."

Whether you're ready to retire or plan to do so in the next few years, you have a unique opportunity. It's your opportunity to recreate yourself through travel, a hobby, something you always wanted to try or haven't done in years. It's your opportunity for personal growth and taking time for yourself, friends, or family.

Whatever you want to do, the future is yours for the taking. This is what a retirement of purpose can be.

But it won't happen without planning.

You need to be financially ready to retire with a clear, defined plan that allows you to live your redesigned future for the rest of your life.

Your plan should consider the best- and worst-case scenarios so you can retire comfortably and maintain your desired lifestyle. It should prepare you both financially and emotionally for inevitable market corrections.

Your retirement plan should also ensure you pay the lowest fees and taxes possible. It needs to consider the timing of events, such as when you'll take withdrawals. It should outline how you will invest allocations of short-term, intermediate-term, and long-term money - including any legacy you want to leave for future generations.

In this book, we'll cover the key aspects of creating a retirement plan that accomplishes all the above.

We'll also look at the steps to finding a well-aligned advisor who works with you personally to not only develop your plan but also to guide you through the inevitable life events that will require you to change, adapt, and reconsider new strategies.

By the end of this book, you'll be ready to design a plan that reflects you and your new future. This is how you will create the retirement you've dreamed of.

So let's get started!

CHAPTER 01

DO YOU HAVE EVERYTHING YOU NEED TO RETIRE? HOW WILL YOU KNOW?

"Your dream retirement depends on how you plan <u>today.</u>"
– Jim Elios

Congratulations! Your hard work, talents, education, and sacrifice have paid off. You're at or near the peak of a successful career that's created a well-deserved lifestyle for you and your family.

Perhaps you've worked with a large, successful company. With the average tenure of management and professional staff ranging from 4.7 to 6.2 years,[1]chances are, you've worked for a few different organizations.

Or perhaps you've built your own successful business or professional practice. Either way, you've worked hard and sacrificed to build your retirement nest egg.

---

[1] News Release Bureau of Labor Statistics, U.S. Department of Labor, Employee Tenure In 2022 PDF

Now what?

With retirement on the horizon, have you thought about how you'll get the most out of your hard-earned savings? Just as important, *have you considered what you'll do after you retire? Do you have a plan? Do you need some guidance and/or inspiration?*

Are You Ready To Retire?

As you near the end of your career, it's normal to feel overwhelmed and even anxious. This is a big shift in your day-to-day life. There are a lot of things to consider. And if you're like most people, you don't know what you don't know. So it's not surprising if you feel uncertain about whether you've made the right assumptions and decisions.

This is when asking the right questions can help you gain clarity. Here are some to consider.

- Are you financially ready to retire? When is your best time to exit? Are you currently on a path to retire on time?
- Do you have a clear and defined retirement plan that will carry you for the rest of your life? Has this plan considered your future goals and potential health scenarios?
- Have you reviewed the best- and worst-case scenarios to retire comfortably and maintain your desired lifestyle?
- Are you financially and emotionally prepared for market corrections?
- Have you taken advantage of tax planning that ensures you pay the least taxes possible? For example, are most of your

retirement assets locked in a 401K subject to increasing taxation as your account grows over time?

- Are your investments and savings keeping pace in a high-inflation environment?
- Do you know where all your retirement accounts are? Are your retirement assets locked in 401k and other tax-qualified accounts? Are they scattered among multiple providers?
- Is your net worth heavily concentrated in specific stocks, and are you not sure how to diversify it?
- Are you concerned about potentially losing your job and the loss of lifestyle that comes with it?
- Will your spouse and/or kids be able to manage your financial affairs if you can't?
- Do you want to preserve and pass on wealth to future generations? What kind of "values" and "valuables" do you want to leave your family?
- Do you have a well-aligned advisor who works with you personally to develop and maintain a solid retirement plan?

In addition to these questions, here is another point to consider.

Where Your Money Is Now May Not Be The Best Long-Term Solution

Are you planning to leave your money where it currently is for retirement?

For example, if you work for a large company, chances are your retirement fund is with a provider such as Fidelity, Vanguard, or a large insurance company. Fidelity Investments is one of the largest financial services companies in the U.S. They work with more than 40 million people and are a dominant player in the 401K and workplace retirement arena. Your 401k or 403B plan may be held there.

If you've accumulated significant retirement savings with Fidelity, you may feel confident about leaving your money there. It's also comfortable if you're used to their dashboard, reports, and so on.

However, firms like Fidelity only handle a part of your financial picture, and most people are unaware of this.

Fidelity will do everything possible to keep you and your money with them. For example, you're 58, working for a company like Progressive Insurance. At this point, Fidelity knows when you're close to retirement. They know how many times you click on their website. They know your assets. They know a lot about you through "data mining" and Artificial Intelligence (AI).

So their AI marketing robot will constantly send you messages, like a dripping faucet. Some messages will tell you to set up a meeting with a planner. You click on a link to arrange a Zoom meeting with a planner who is hundreds of miles away. You may never speak with someone locally.

Chances are, you will work with three to five representatives throughout your retirement. You won't have an advisor who gets to know you and forms a personal commitment to you and your family.

Just as important, Fidelity will not work with you to provide a comprehensive retirement plan. Why? Because they are an investment provider, not a financial advisor, and it's important to separate the two.

For example, a Fidelity representative cannot give you tax advice. While they have lots of tools to manage money, they want to avoid liability when it comes to taxes. A financial advisor, on the other hand, will give you the advice you need.

A planner working with a firm like Fidelity will likely recommend their proprietary investments. Meanwhile, several other options on the market are as good or better. You can get these options with an experienced advisor, especially with one who is a designated fiduciary.

My overriding point is this: A provider like Fidelity cannot provide the comprehensive personal service or objective and independent advice that you get from a fiduciary financial planner.

Overall, workplace 401K plans are solid accumulation vehicles, whether you're with Fidelity or another investment company. They're an excellent place to start while you're "climbing the mountain" to retirement. However, getting down the retirement mountain is entirely different because you are looking at something far more complicated than pulling money out of your 401K.

Let's take a look at why.

Are You Maximizing Your Company Retirement Plans?

One of the most important things you can do is to maximize your company's retirement benefits. Yet many people fail to do this because they don't know what their benefit plan offers. At the minimum, you should plan to contribute enough to receive the company match.

An example of an additional benefit that is often not clearly communicated or understood can be found in the Cleveland Clinic's retirement plan. This plan offers a unique opportunity to take advantage of a "Mega backdoor Roth," which is important if you earn an above-average income.

Traditional Roth IRAs allow you to contribute money after paying income tax. These dollars can then grow tax-free. However, income rules restrict who can contribute to a Roth. Plus, as of 2024, there was a maximum IRA contribution limit of $7,000 if you were under 50 or $8,000 if you were older.

A mega backdoor Roth is ideal for people with a 401(k) plan, like the one provided by Cleveland Clinic. In 2024, staff were able to put up to $46,000 of their post-tax dollars into their 401(k) plan and then roll it into a mega backdoor Roth, in either a Roth IRA or Roth 401(k).[2]

However, creating a mega backdoor Roth is complicated. One mistake can mean you'll be hit with an unexpected tax bill. So, working with a

[2] https://www.nerdwallet.com/article/investing/mega-backdoor-roths-work

trusted financial advisor is essential before you take advantage of it.

In fact, a financial advisor can ensure that you take advantage of every benefit your company retirement plan offers, no matter where you work.

Are You Ready For The Descent Down The Retirement Mountain?

The journey down is far more complicated than the ascent, whether you're descending into retirement or descending an actual mountain.

A study looked at all Everest climbs between 1921 and 2006. Some 192 of the 212 deaths on the mountain occurred above the final base camp at 26,246 feet. Among the climbers who died, 56 percent passed on their *descent* from Everest's summit, while another 17 percent died after turning back. Only 15 percent died on the way up or before leaving their final camp. [3]

What's interesting is getting to the top of Mount Everest takes about six weeks. This gives climbers time to acclimate to the high altitude. However, that's also a long time for accidents to happen. On the other hand, descending from the summit to base camp only takes a couple of days. Yet the bulk of deaths occur in this period.

---

[3] https://www.scientificamerican.com/blog/news-blog/death-on-mount-everest-the-perils-o-2008-12-10/

Why? Climbers often give everything they've got to reach the summit. They simply have nothing left in the tank to climb down. Sometimes, they succumb to altitude sickness. Or they make mistakes due to exhaustion.

In some ways, our working and retirement lives are similar. We climb the mountain, working hard, saving, and planning to build our retirement nest egg. And we do this for the majority of our lives.

When we reach the peak, we feel the exhilaration of freedom. Now, we have time to do what we always wanted, right?

But we often don't plan for our "descent" down the mountain. In other words, we don't have a plan for maximizing and organizing retirement funds, fulfilling our goals, and staying healthy. Even worse, we make mistakes that can cost us financial security.

Here are some of the most common mistakes I see retirees make:

Falling into recency bias

This bias causes us to think that recent events will likely happen again soon. Instead of having a long-term view, we ignore statistical probability and history and overemphasize fresh experiences in our memory.

A perfect example of this was the 2022 stock market decline. The S&P 500 lost 18.32% that year, and the tech-heavy NASDAQ 100 index fared much worse, plummeting 33% in its worst performance since 2008.

Not surprisingly, some people pulled their money out of stocks, stashing it in cash or money markets. Many did this after their stock values had already dropped. Even worse, they missed the rebound in 2023, so they lost even more money.

By the end of 2023's first quarter, the S&P had gained 5.5%. By the start of 2024, this gain was more than 24%. And this rebound wasn't limited to the S&P 500. By January 25th, the Dow Jones Industrial Average closed above 38,000 for the first time, while the Nasdaq saw its highest close in two years on January 29th. People who had pulled out of stocks in mid to late 2022 missed this rally.

Not understanding tax laws with resulting high taxes on withdrawals

While many people understand the markets and investments, they often don't understand taxes. Yet saving money in taxes equates to longer-term wealth.

One of the biggest mistakes I see is having too much of your net worth in qualified or pre-tax funds like 401Ks. If this is your situation, you can kiss 30% of this money goodbye, thanks to taxes.

Paying high fees

There is a complete lack of transparency in the financial investment industry when it comes to fees. Many retirees are surprised to hear of hidden costs in their investments. Some investments, like variable annuities and certain mutual funds, have much higher costs than similar exchange-traded funds, or ETFs.

Knowing your fees is important because lower fees translate to better long-term returns. The lower your costs, the better your results will be. This chart from the Securities and Exchange Commission, or SEC, illustrates this impact well.

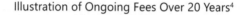

Illustration of Ongoing Fees Over 20 Years[4]

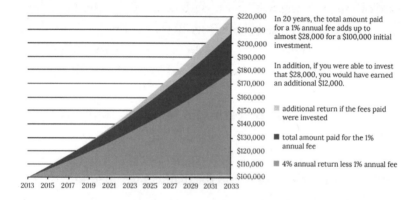

In 20 years, the total amount paid for a 1% annual fee adds up to almost $28,000 for a $100,000 initial investment.

In addition, if you were able to invest that $28,000, you would have earned an additional $12,000.

■ additional return if the fees paid were invested

■ total amount paid for the 1% annual fee

■ 4% annual return less 1% annual fee

Making short-term decisions for long-term investments

Many people make short-term decisions to manage long-term investments. This means the bulk of their money is not set up to handle economic downturns and market shifts.

Your long-term money should be properly diversified and positioned for long-term growth above the inflation rate. When done right, diversification works over time to increase your returns while managing risk.

---

4   https://www.sec.gov/investor/alerts/ib_fees_expenses.pdf

Leaving health out of your retirement plan

When it comes to planning your retirement, health is an important consideration. By 2021, the average American lived for 76.1 years, which means people are living longer. Yet many people do not think about this properly, and this is when they can run out of money.

Of course, no one can predict how long you'll live. But a solid retirement plan allows for a long life expectancy so you can live comfortably. It also has provisions for the extra costs that can help you heal from an unexpected illness or injury so you can enjoy the rest of the time you have.

If you feel you're making any of these mistakes now or are unsure, you still have time to change course and get your retirement on track. In the chapters ahead, I'll show you how to avoid these mistakes so you can enjoy the retirement you've always dreamed of.

If you would like more information on planning your enlightened retirement, visit https://www.eliosfinancial.com

CHAPTER 02

STRONG PRINCIPLES LEAD TO SOLID RETIREMENT PLANNING

"Everything I learned about being a financial advisor came from having an "old school" paper route—it's about customer service and managing money!"

– Jim Elios

Like most people, my parents greatly influenced my life. Their love, guidance, and discipline brought me to where I am today.

In fact, everything we'll cover in this book is based on the solid foundation of principles and purpose they gave me. With this foundation, I've created principles or axioms that guide me in creating stronger relationships and financial plans for my clients.

And it all started with a man who immigrated from Greece to the United States, looking for a better life.

A Strong Foundation

My dad, Thomas Eliopoulos, was born in 1930 in a small rural village in northern Greece called Velventos. When he was just 11 years old, in April 1941, Nazi Germany invaded Greece, overrunning the country in just a month. In that same year, his dad, my grandfather, died suddenly from untreated appendicitis, leaving my grandmother, my dad, and his three sisters on their own.

Overall, life in Northern Greece during the German invasion was characterized by fear, uncertainty, and hardship as civilians grappled with the realities of war and occupation. Despite the challenges, many individuals and communities demonstrated resilience and courage in the face of adversity, which contributed to the eventual liberation of Greece from Axis control.

My dad's family experienced hardship throughout this time, and my father was determined to improve his and his family's lives. He finished 6th grade and worked odd jobs to support his Mom (my Yia Yia) and three sisters. Northern Greece is known for its rich, fertile valleys, especially for its peach orchards. He worked in the fields as well as in shipping for a fruit cooperative.

As soon as he was 18, my dad joined the Greek army, where he eventually rose to the rank of captain. But even then, he realized there had to be something better. This was when he began to think about immigrating to the United States.

Thomas Elios 1948 Greek Army

He had a great uncle who lived in Flint, Michigan. So in 1954, he struck out on his own, traveling over 6,000 miles by ship, plane, and bus to Flint. His first job was in a restaurant, where he worked hard to save money. From there, he moved to Cleveland, Ohio, in part to join friends who had also emigrated from the same village in Greece but also because he thought there was more opportunity there. Cleveland was a thriving industrial city with automotive and steel companies employing many in the post-WW2 era.

For the first few years, my dad worked for several restaurants in Cleveland and rented a one-room apartment in a neighborhood called Archwood-Denison. He diligently saved everything he could while making ends meet. Then, in 1961, he fulfilled his promise to a patient fiancee and returned to Greece to marry my

Mom. He brought her back to Cleveland, where they started a family in 1961.

1961 Wedding Velventos Greece

Since he was so poor as a child, my dad had a scarcity mindset. But he was also willing to take a risk. He knew he wanted a better life. That's why he left everything to move to the United States, to pursue the American Dream, just as millions of other Americans have done.

By working hard, he found his version of the American dream by becoming a successful restaurant owner. This alone was inspirational to me. But my parents also instilled three important values when it comes to money:

Save money for a rainy day:

Having a reserve of money, along with a plan on when and how you'll use it, gives you freedom and peace of mind. This mindset allowed me to save money for my college education while I was in high school.

Education is key:

Learning and keeping an open mind will lead you to a career, opportunity, or business where you can start a family, save, and build wealth. My parents supported and encouraged me to do my best throughout my schooling. As a result, My siblings and I were the first in my family to get a college degree, and I went on to get a Master's degree in business.

Connect and serve people:

Building relationships leads to opportunities to help others, who in turn help you. One of the best ways I learned the value of this principle was through my part-time jobs.

How Delivering Newspapers Taught Me To Be A Good Financial Advisor

At around the age of 12, I started cutting grass and delivering newspapers. Both jobs gave me vital lessons in service and being an "entrepreneur"- especially the newspaper route I managed. In the summer of 1978, a neighborhood kid quit his route and offered it to me. I gladly accepted the job for an opportunity to make money so I could buy - of all things - baseball cards! I began delivering the *Cleveland Press*, which was published in the afternoon. This allowed me to deliver papers after I got home from school.

Long before cable TV, the internet, social media, and AI, newspapers were the primary source of information and news. People loved reading the paper and depended on it for daily news, sports, and weather. Having a paper route was an opportunity to provide a valuable service. It put some money in my pocket and was a great way to keep up on daily news and follow my life-long favorite baseball team, the Cleveland Indians (now Guardians).

The interesting concept with delivering papers is that you must buy them from the publisher first. So, with a route of 100 households, I would buy 100 papers for a "wholesale" price. Then, I had to deliver the papers and collect a "retail price" from my customers. This was a true lesson in "Business 101": Buy wholesale and sell retail.

It didn't take me long to discover that customers had specific service needs and expectations. For example, some wanted their paper behind the screen door, others on their porch, and still others in their mailbox. I soon realized that by giving the customers what they wanted, I could do better, too.

Every week, I would make the rounds to collect the newspaper fees from my customers. If I did a good job, I'd get a tip. This taught me the value of being dependable, friendly, on-time, and diligent about details. I carry this lesson into my professional life to this day!

But that's not all my paper route taught me.

My paper route and lawn mowing jobs allowed me to save money. And my dad encouraged this, too. When I wanted that shiny new bike I saw in the department store, for example, he would offer to pay for half if I came up with the other half. It didn't take me long to see the value of savings (and a dollar-for-dollar match)!

I opened my first bank account and would make weekly deposits at the bank (riding my new shiny bike!) This was like a precursor of a 401K, and it gave me the excitement of seeing my money grow. I still do this today and have shown my three kids the wonder of compounding interest!

When I was in high school, I became interested in stocks. My friends and I would pretend to be professional "stock pickers" on Wall Street, looking at the stock tables that were published daily and randomly picking the winners. But this was the early 1980s, and stock investing was only for the "wealthy."

In 1988, I graduated from Bowling Green State University in Bowling Green, Ohio, with a degree in Marketing and Finance. I then went to work for a large bank called National City Bank, which started in 1845 in Cleveland (now part of PNC Bank). It was interesting how this bank survived the Great Depression yet went bankrupt in the greedy 2000s when it made "subprime" loans to unqualified buyers.

However, I left National City before this happened to work for a large financial services company. This required me to work with different banks and travel throughout Ohio.

Then, in 1995, the year I married Solveig Anna Miesen, I started my career as a personal financial advisor, training in all aspects of financial planning for the Cleveland Financial Group/Lincoln

Financial Advisors. This was perfect for me because I was a good saver and investor. Plus, I loved working with people. Even so, I still wanted to have my own business, like my dad.

So, in 2001, I formed the Elios Financial Group. When I wrote this book, we managed $300M for over 250 families - teaching prosperity and purpose daily and delivering the same kind of service I learned as a paperboy!

A Financial Service Based On Knowledge, Integrity, and Relationships

When I started my business, I knew relationships with people and money were core. This led to my mission and vision for my business:

Our Purpose:
We build long-term relationships by helping clients envision their dreams, enlighten them to make informed financial decisions through education, and provide service that ultimately enriches their lives.

Our Vision:
To be the most trusted advisor for clients using our professional knowledge, integrity, and personalized service.

To accomplish this, everyone in my firm lives by the premise of "Envision, Enlighten, and Enrich."

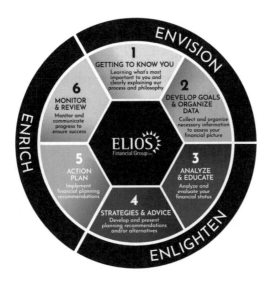

With my upbringing, experience, and education forming the foundation, I developed the Elios' Axioms. I chose the word "axiom" because it's defined as a statement or proposition that is regarded as being established, accepted, or self-evidently true. So, the axioms I work with are widely considered to be truisms, self-evident, and established proven principles that have worked for me and my clients for the past 28 years.

As we go through these axioms in this book, I'll show you how they can help you enjoy retirement:

- Successful investing outcomes are directly related to an investor's behavior, every time. We'll talk about this in the next chapter.
- No one can predict the future or control the financial markets. However, we can control the risk-adjusted vehicles to invest your money. I'll show you some of the best ways to do this in Chapter 4.

- Never make short-term decisions on money set aside for the long term. Equally important, don't make long-term decisions on the money you're using for the short term. We'll cover this in Chapter 5.

- Cash and liquidity are always your first consideration. You'll see the best investment vehicles for your cash in Chapter 5, along with options for your intermediate and longer-term investments.

- Saving money in taxes equates to greater long-term wealth. I'll show you some ways you can pay less taxes in Chapter 6.

- Diversification works over the long term. We'll get into diversification and how to do it in Chapter 7.

- The lower fees you pay, the better returns you'll get. You'll see how you can lower fees in Chapter 7.

- We match up your time horizon and your expectations to manage risk. Chapter 7 will also include risk management options.

- Health above wealth always. Without health, what good is your money? I'll give you ideas to consider for your retirement plan in Chapter 9.

- As a fiduciary, we align with your best interests. It's a legal higher standard of care. And just as important, the better you do, the better we do. We'll cover this and how to pick the right advisor for you in Chapter 10.

Now, let's look at how these axioms can help you and your family.

CHAPTER 03

SUCCESSFUL INVESTING IS DIRECTLY RELATED TO YOUR BEHAVIOR

"Separate your investments from the winds of political bias, herd mentality, and emotions. Stay disciplined, and the stock market will reward you well. History proves it."
– Jim Elios

If there's one tendency that we humans share, it's making decisions based on emotions. So, when it comes to money, emotions cause us to make irrational decisions. And that can be costly.

Over the years, I have found that some clients consistently want to make the wrong moves at the wrong times. Now, they're smart people with successful careers and lives. But inevitably, they want to buy more stocks when the market is at an all-time high.

This is absolutely the wrong time. Buying when the market or a stock is at an all-time high is when you face the greatest risk for loss. But the excitement of making big gains with a high-flying stock takes over rational thinking. We can't get around the fact that we are emotional beings who make emotional decisions.

So why does this happen, and is there anything we can do about it? Let's examine the situation.

Why Your Mindset Matters - The Science of Behavioral Finance

Behavioral Economics and its subfield, Behavioral Finance, are important areas of academic study, for good reason. I'll give you examples of why in a moment, but let's take a look at the definitions first.

Investopedia defines Behavioral Economics as the "study of psychology as it relates to the economic decision-making processes of individuals and institutions." For example, companies use behavioral economics to develop their marketing, price their products, and even design their packaging.[5]

---

[5] https://www.investopedia.com/terms/b/behavioraleconomics.asp

Behavioral Finance narrows the study down to focusing on how psychological influences can affect investor behavior and, as a result, market outcomes.[6] As I mentioned, this is a significant field of study in the academic world. In fact, Dr. Richard H. Thaler won a Nobel Prize for "his contributions to behavioral economics" in 2017.[7] But why is this topic so important to you?

Behavioral finance relates to mindset, which you develop based on a wide range of factors, including your upbringing, past experiences, and culture. You could say your mindset rules your life because it affects your emotions, biases, and behaviors.

Most of us don't even think about why we make certain decisions. Yet, all of your decisions are affected by your mindset. You can make mistakes if you're unaware of how your mindset guides your decision-making.

For example, one behavioral finance tenant is called "recency bias." This bias causes us to assume that future events will resemble recent experiences. In other words, we believe that if certain events happened recently, they are likely to happen again soon. So, unless we're aware of this bias, we make decisions accordingly.

Here is a sports example: The debate over whether LeBron James is better than Michael Jordan is often influenced by recency bias, especially among younger fans or those who didn't watch Jordan play during his prime.

---

[6] https://www.investopedia.com/terms/b/behavioralfinance.asp

[7] https://www.nobelprize.org/prizes/economic-sciences/2017/thaler/facts/

LeBron has dominated the NBA for nearly two decades, and his longevity and current performances are fresh in people's minds. This can lead some to argue that LeBron is the greatest because they witness his achievements in real time. On the other hand, those who grew up watching Jordan often argue that his six championships, scoring titles, and clutch performances make him the GOAT (Greatest of All Time).

Recency bias comes into play when people put more weight on LeBron's recent accomplishments, like his continued dominance into his late 30s, while downplaying or forgetting Jordan's legacy, which includes different contexts, like the style of play and level of competition in the 1990s. This doesn't mean one is definitively better than the other, but the bias can sway opinions based on what's happening now rather than the full picture of their careers.

Here's another example: Let's say you're interviewing candidates for a job. The last candidate you interview impresses you the most because they have an excellent presentation and seem very knowledgeable. As a result, you might be inclined to rate them higher and remember them more favorably than earlier candidates, even if some earlier candidates were equally or more qualified. This bias can influence your decision-making process, potentially leading you to overlook important factors or make suboptimal choices.

In investment terms, recency bias can manifest when investors make decisions based on recent market trends or performance rather than considering the long-term fundamentals of an investment. For instance, if a particular stock has performed exceptionally well in the past few weeks, investors might be tempted to buy more of it, assuming that the trend will continue, without thoroughly analyzing the underlying reasons for the recent performance.

As I mentioned earlier, many investors experienced this when they sold stocks in the summer of 2022, believing the market would continue to decline.

Rather than stepping back to examine statistical probabilities and history, they overemphasized recent experience. So, they sold their stocks at a loss and then missed the rally that followed in 2023. This was a costly mistake.

We also saw this in the 2002 "tech wreck." Millions of investors became disillusioned and dropped out of the market. Unfortunately, they didn't get back into it until several years later (if at all), when it had already made significant gains.

The same happened more recently with Bitcoin in 2021. After plunging to a price of less than $4,000 at the start of the pandemic, Bitcoin began to climb. By November 2021, it closed at an all-time high of $69,000. Investors piled in to get a piece of the action.

However, Bitcoin began to drop again in early 2022. By the middle of June 2022, it had fallen to $20,000. Scores of investors who had bought high sold low for a significant loss.[8] One thing to note is that if they had held on, Bitcoin was hovering at around $70,000 as of June 2024.

---

[8] https://www.forbes.com/advisor/investing/cryptocurrency/bitcoin-price-history/

Recency bias isn't the only behavior that affects your mindset when it comes to investments. Your mindset will also determine whether you participate in situations caused by herd mentality.[9] This happens when people adopt the beliefs, behaviors, or attitudes of the majority in a group, even at the expense of their own judgment.

You see herd mentality every day, from fashion trends to political movements and, of course, with investment decisions.

Herd mentality causes stock bubbles, like the dot-com and housing bubbles we experienced in the 2000's. Both led to significant market crashes. And I don't think anyone will forget the recent example of people rushing to buy toilet paper during the pandemic! Remember the handmade masks we were wearing?

The most important thing is recognizing that mindset affects our view of events and situations. This can lead to irrational decisions that negatively impact our lives.

This is why I want to discuss another fundamental mindset of scarcity versus abundance, which can greatly affect your financial success.

Scarcity vs. Abundance - Which Belief Do You Have?

The old saying, "Viewing the glass as half-empty instead of half-full," is a good analogy for a scarcity mindset. But how do you know if you fall into the "half-empty" category?

---

[9] https://www.verywellmind.com/how-herd-mentality-explains-our-behavior-7487018

Here are three things to watch for.

First, you may feel fear more often than optimism if you have a scarcity mindset. If you find yourself saying things like, "The world is going to hell. The market's going to crash. Our debt will cause society to collapse. We're going to have another depression.", then you probably have a scarcity mindset. Media sources often perpetuate scarcity by promoting fear. In other words, they cater to the fear in viewers, which is a perfect example of confirmation bias.

Second, you may watch or follow daily news that is biased toward the negative or "fear." This can cause you to react to events rather than figure out how to handle them. You fall into a reactionary mindset where you might buy gold, stay too cash-heavy, pull money out of the stock market, or buy an illiquid annuity that pays less than 4%. In other words, you make quick decisions that don't align with your long-term goals based on a scarcity or risk-averse emotion.

Finally, you believe life is a zero-sum game: "If I win, you lose." This contradicts the win-win belief where both people mutually benefit and enjoy abundance.

If you see yourself in any or all of these examples, it's OK. Recognizing that you have this belief makes it easier to understand that you can react differently in the future.

Look, we are all human, and at some point, we all experience fear. Sometimes, especially in the short term, a scarcity mindset can benefit you. But when we're talking about your long-term money, you need to step back and acknowledge your mindset before making financial decisions. Doing the right things over time will lead to abundance!

Finally, politics is another important area where you must separate beliefs from your money.

Why You Need To Avoid The Politics Of Money

As I write this, we are facing another election year, and it appears it will be a repeat of 2020 election. So when I talk with different investors, I hear it all:

"Well, if we have another four years of Biden, I'm cashing out of stocks." Or, "If Trump's elected, I'm moving to Canada."

Since 1928, we've had many presidents. But look at the trajectory of the markets in the same time period. Over time, whether the president was a Democrat or Republican, markets went up. While it may seem hard to believe, the president had little impact on the stock market. The graph below illustrates this perfectly.

The U.S. economy has continued to grow regardless of who is in the White House

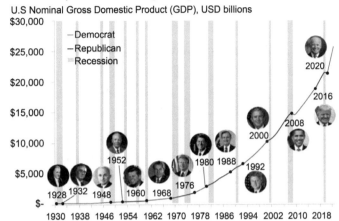

U.S Nominal Gross Domestic Product (GDP), USD billions

Source: BEA, Haver Analytics, White House History. J.P. Morgan Wealth Management. Data as of Q3 2023. Party indicator is that the serving president at that time. Markers only represent election years (intra-term presidents not pictured).

In fact, the president has a limited impact on the economy overall. Sure, they can create an environment that is better or worse for the economy, but either way, the market keeps climbing over time.

My takeaway is this: It's the United States of America! We have a free market at the center of our institutions. Yes, it is free enterprise and capitalism that provide a dynamic economy with opportunities for growth and innovation in companies. In the last 20 years, we have created Smartphones, EVs, cloud computing, and even gene-sequencing technology.

These innovations have created enormous economic value. Think of companies like Apple, Google, Meta, Tesla, Nvidia, Eli Lilly, etc. Of the top ten biggest companies in the world, nine out of ten are American companies. It is our institutions of freedom, innovation, and education system that have manifested an economy of valuable companies with rising valuations. Politicians can foster an environment for a good economy, but in my opinion, not directly.

Of course, politicians will try to take credit for a rising market if they are the party in power. But it's not the Republicans or Democrats who created Artificial Intelligence, electric cars, cloud computing, and life-saving drugs. It was entrepreneurs, scientists, engineers, and educators - individuals empowered by our economy. And this will never change.

As a sports reference - politicians taking credit for the economy is similar to a football quarterback. They get all the credit when the team wins and all the blame when they lose. This greatly oversimplifies the game!

Election cycles come and go, along with politicians. So, basing your long-term investment and retirement plan on short-term elections and policies is not a good strategy. Don't make the mistake of tying your political views with your investments because you will make errors and miss out on opportunities.

What's most important about your mindset is to recognize that you have certain emotions and biases. When you see this, it's easier to separate emotions from your decisions.

For example, when you understand herd mentality, you can see when it's happening and then make more informed choices. The graph below shows how avoiding herd mentality and staying the course creates better results.

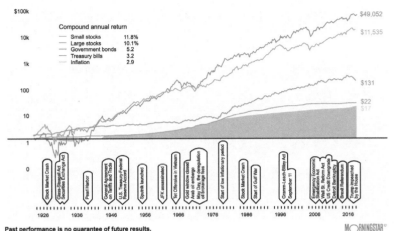

Past performance is no guarantee of future results,

Past performance is no guarantee of future results. Hypothetical value of $1 invested at the beginning of 1926. Assumes reinvestment of income and no transaction cost or taxes. This is for illustrative purposes only and not indicative of any investment. An investment cannot be made directly in an index. © Morningstar 2023 and Precision Information, dba Financial fitness Group 2023. All Rights Reserved.

This is why having a well-thought-out financial and retirement plan is so important. It's also critical to work with an advisor you trust so you can talk with him or her *before* you make any decision.

Look, we are all human. It's not always easy to control behavior, especially when your emotions are screaming at you, telling you to do something different.

But in the end, controlling your emotions and following your plan pays off. History proves it. Stocks have well-rewarded, disciplined investors for decades.

If you would like to see how my team can help you develop a plan to guide you through market ups and downs, contact us at https://www.eliosfinancial.com for a complimentary appointment.

CHAPTER 04

FOCUS ON WHAT YOU CAN CONTROL FOR A LONG, HAPPY RETIREMENT

"Retirement is wonderful. It's doing nothing without worrying about getting caught at it."
– Gene Perret, *American comedy writer and producer*

Although it would be nice if we could, no one can predict the future or control financial markets.

There will always be reasons not to invest. We can't control the election. We can't control interest rates. We can't control climate change. The list goes on and on.

Whatever it may be, there will always be reasons not to invest in the markets. But if you focus on this, you will never succeed as you should. So, let's quiet the noise and focus on what we *can* control.

We can look at how you plan to spend and save money. We can time certain events and actions both before and after retirement to cut investment costs and taxes. We can focus on strategies to reduce risk and help your investments grow. And we can explore the best opportunities to leave a legacy.

Let's examine these five factors—Spending, Saving, Timing, Risk, and Legacy—and how they impact retirement planning.

5 Factors You Can Control To Protect And Grow Your Money

Spending

According to financial blogger Avraham Byers, spending is about bringing the right level of consciousness and awareness to how you use and save your money. By doing this, you spend money only on things that truly enrich your life and nothing on things that bring you feelings of guilt or shame. Great definition.

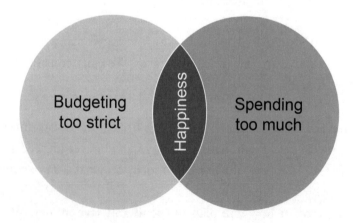

When it comes to spending, most financial advisors plan for a 30-year retirement window. So, in the traditional planning view, they look at three spending phases, at 10 years each, for retirement: Go-Go, Slow-Go, and No-Go.

So what the heck does this mean?

The Go-Go phase is your first decade of retirement. According to planners, this is when you'll pursue hobbies, travel, make new friends, and perhaps buy a new house or relocate. This is considered the fun years of retirement and often the most expensive period.

In your second decade, or the Go-Slow period, planners expect you to spend less. This might mean traveling less, moving closer to family and friends, and slowing down overall. You may even downsize to one vehicle!

Finally, in the third stage of No-Go, you're now in your eighties or nineties. This is when your resources go to making your life as comfortable and healthy for as long as possible. In traditional planning, this means you're not spending as much, but you have resources available in case you need extra care.

As I mentioned, this is the traditional view of retirement planning. However, I like to plan for Go-Go for your entire retirement. Yes, you may go through all three stages, but why not plan to enjoy your retirement to its fullest for your entire life?

What we can control is your spending plan. We can match your goals with your finances to guide you on what to spend so you don't run out of money.

Savings

Your savings are money dedicated to your peace of mind, emergencies, and liquid funds. So, it's essential to protect your savings while also allowing your money to grow. While no one can guarantee total safety for your money, you can control how you invest it and in what amounts. We will explore this in greater detail in Chapter 7.

The main point I want to make now is that you must keep an adequate amount of cash and liquid investments on hand. This is your emergency reserve fund, and it's critical to have, whether retirement is still down the road or you're already there.

A good rule of thumb is to dedicate 3-5% of your overall funds to your reserves. Another way to look at this is to set aside a year of living expenses. There are several reasons why this is so important.

For instance, if you planned to retire in 2022, you faced a dilemma. 2022 was a lousy year to retire because markets dropped significantly. If you had to withdraw money for retirement in 2022, you may have been forced to pull from an account that was down 10-15%, maybe more.

To avoid this, you would have had two options: delay retirement or use your cash on hand.

If you had enough cash, you could have still retired and used this money to live on. You wouldn't have been forced to withdraw from investments when markets temporarily declined. This is a much better position to be in.

In the past, cash was considered dead money. But today, there are several short-term vehicles where you can keep some of your cash reserves and actually make a bit of money. We will talk more about this in the next chapter.

Overall, it's essential to know that you can control how you save money so that it lasts the rest of your life.

Timing

We can control the timing of specific steps, both before and after retiring. The first example of timing is considering when you're going to retire. This decision also depends on when you plan to take Social Security or Medicare.

I call this Critical Age-Based Planning because the timing of these steps can save you money—and sometimes, lots of money. The illustration below shows some of the most important steps.

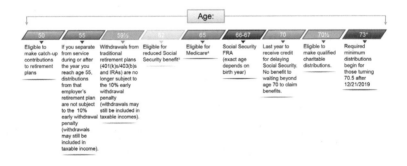

* In 2033, the age goes to 75.

For example, early withdrawals from traditional retirement plans, like 401(k)s/403(b)s and IRAs, are subject to a 10% penalty. So, deciding when to take withdrawals is critical for your retirement plan. Conversely, all funds qualified for retirement with pre-tax dollars require you to make lifetime withdrawals or Required Minimum Withdrawals (RMDs).

Risk

You can control which risk-adjusted vehicles you invest your money in. The bottom line is you want to take the minimum risk needed to maximize your long-term goals.

Controlling risk includes managing the time horizon of your money. For example, your emergency reserve fund should be kept in liquid, very low-risk investments. On the other hand, your long-term money can be invested in growth stocks, with just enough risk to allow your funds to grow.

Managing time horizons is not a common practice when it comes to retirement. So, we'll cover this in detail in the next chapter.

Legacy

Finally, you can also control your legacy. Whether you want to leave as much money as possible for your heirs or none at all, this decision is up to you.

You can decide what to leave your heirs, including whether you want to give them money before your passing. You can also choose to fund charities or other organizations. You can also take steps to minimize the costs of estate and probate taxes.

You've now seen five factors that are under your control when investing and planning your retirement.

Next, we'll examine how you can work with each factor to protect and grow your money.

If you would like help reviewing your retirement plan, reach out to us at https://www.eliosfinancial.com to arrange a complimentary appointment.

CHAPTER 05

DON'T MAKE SHORT-TERM DECISIONS ON LONG-TERM MONEY - DON'T MAKE LONG-TERM DECISIONS ON SHORT-TERM MONEY

"When it comes to retirement, one of the biggest mistakes I see is people retiring with almost all their money in a 401K."

– Jim Elios

I was working in my office one morning when the phone rang. The caller was one of my clients, Todd. After exchanging "Hellos" and family updates, I asked what was on his mind.

"Jim, I've got to get out of the stock market. I can't stand it any longer!"I was shocked, to say the least. "Todd, I didn't know you were planning to retire next year! He replied, "Oh no, I'm not retiring for another 10 or 15 years. I just want to get out and protect my money."

Todd was falling into the trap of making a short-term decision for money he wouldn't need for a long time. This is why it's essential to match up what you need your money for with your time horizon. Besides, getting out of the market requires two decisions: when to get out and even more difficult, when to get back in!

Sounds simple, right? However, consider behavioral finance, which I mentioned earlier. It's easy to get caught in emotions and make wrong decisions for your investments.

When it comes to managing your money, you need to consider three time horizons: Short-Term, Intermediate, and Long-Term. In other words, you should have three "buckets" of money managed according to each time horizon.

Yet when I meet new clients, I find that many have nearly all their savings in a long-term investment, like a 401K. Anything left over is usually a small pot of cash. This is not the ideal way to approach retirement. So, let's review these three money buckets and why you'll need them.

Client: Example
Date: 1/18/2024

Asset Location, Time Horizon and Taxes

	Potential Needs	Investment Vehicles	Account Type	Taxation	Risk Level	Value
Short-term 0 - 12 Months	Emergency Reserves Living Expenses Capital Purchases Vacation Taxes	Money Markets Short Term Bonds Cash or Certificate of Deposit or CD	Checking/Savings Money Market Accounts	Ordinary Income	Low to none	$
Intermediate 3-10 years	Capital Purchases Vehicles Home Renovation Projects Education Healthcare Costs	Tax-Free Municipal Bonds Corporate Bonds Dividend Stocks Growth Stocks and ETF's Master Limited Partnerships or MLP's Real Estate Investment Trusts or REITS	Brokerage Account Investment Account 529 Plan Trust Account	Capital Gains Dividends 0% 15% 20%	Moderate	$
Long Term 10+ years	Retirement Income Heatheare Costs Long Term Care Estate	Dividend Stocks Growth Stocks and ETF's Real Estate Investment Trusts or REITS	401(k) - IRA's ROTH IRA's Annuities Brokerage Account Trust Accounts Life Insurance	All Qualified: 403b/401k IRA's Roth IRA's Annuities Brokerage Accounts Trust Accounts Cash Value Life Insurance	Growth Tax Free Acc $ $	$ $
					Total:	$

Rev: 1/2024

Short Term: Liquid Assets

As you can see in the graph above, short-term cash is the money you'll need in the next 12 months. This is the liquid part of your portfolio. The goal is to keep this money safe, so none of it should be in stock markets.

Again, in the past, we called cash dead money, but not anymore. Today, you can make 5% on cash in money markets with little risk. A money market is an excellent place to park money for the short term.

Intermediate: Your investment portfolio

Your intermediate money is actually your investment portfolio. It is *not* your retirement money or your cash.

If this sounds confusing, I get it.

Your retirement money is in the long-term bucket with your 401 (k), IRA, Roth IRA, or long-term annuities. These are your retirement and income-producing assets.

On the other hand, the intermediate bucket is a taxable investment portfolio. This portfolio allows you to diversify your investments. Your money can grow more than it would in a short-term investment, yet it's still liquid.

One thing to note is that these intermediate investments have beneficial tax implications. This topic is so important that I've devoted the next chapter to it.

Another note I want to mention is the 529 Plan. A 529 plan allows you to save money for education, including costs for kindergarten through grade 12, apprenticeship programs, and college. Since it's a tax-deferred account, your savings are not taxed. Even better, withdrawals are tax-free as long as they're used for qualified education expenses.

So, a 529 can be very important if you have kids who will be going to college or are attending now like I have today. (Thank you, Miami University, Ohio State, and Virginia Tech!) You can pay the school directly or reimburse yourself for eligible education costs and pay NO taxes on gains. And thanks to the Setting Every Community Up for Retirement Enhancement Act of 2019 (SECURE Act) along with the amendment to this Act in 2022, 529s can also be used to pay off student loans or fund a Roth IRA.[10]

Long-term: Retirement Money

Finally, your third bucket of money is your retirement nest egg. Generally speaking, most people have this money in qualified retirement vehicles like 401Ks or 403Bs, annuities, and IRAs.

This is your long-term money, whether you're 50 or 70. You need this money to last the rest of your life, so we invest for growth and income. The ROTH IRA should be your longest-term asset, even longer-term than an IRA. And because all growth and withdrawals are tax-free, you may want this to be your most aggressive (all-stock) asset.

You now have an overview of the three money buckets you'll need for retirement. As I mentioned earlier, tax implications for each bucket are significant, to say the least. The steps you take in managing your money can save you thousands of dollars or cost you plenty. In the next chapter, you'll see why.

I have a checklist on my website to help you take an inventory of the money you have invested for the short, intermediate, and long term. You can download yours at https://www.eliosfinancial.com

---

[10] https://www.investopedia.com/terms/1/529plan.asp

CHAPTER 06

HOW SAVING ON TAXES INCREASES LONG-TERM WEALTH

"Our new Constitution is now established; everything seems to promise it will be durable; but, in this world, nothing is certain except death and taxes."

– Benjamin Franklin

I am just like everybody, I hate to pay taxes!

But of course, it's the law. As Oliver Wendell Holmes wrote, "Taxes are the price of a civilized society." We simply can't avoid them. And it shocks many of my clients to learn that their tax bracket could be higher at age 80 than in their final year of work.

This is why knowing how your investments are taxed and the implications of withdrawing money is essential. That way, you can develop a plan that could literally save you hundreds of thousands of dollars and possibly more.

Plus, since tax laws are incredibly complex, working with an expert is vital to developing your tax plan. However, the person you may view as an expert might not be someone you should work with.

Who You Use To Prepare Your Taxes Probably Can't Help You With Tax Planning

When you think about it, most tax preparers are historians. They look at what happened last year and then check the boxes on your tax forms, with the result being that you hopefully stay even with the IRS and don't overpay.

This is the process for filing taxes. However, for tax planning, you need to look into the future and consider several options to mitigate the taxes you will pay. This is a whole different ball game.

Now, some CPAs do this, but not all. We've already discussed how a firm like Fidelity will manage workplace retirement accounts but will not take the liability of giving tax advice. Tax planning is simply a service they don't provide.

So, who do you talk to?

This is when you need to talk with a financial advisor who is well-versed in the tax code and how retirement and investments are taxed. A good advisor can look at your current financial situation and then, based on this, make assumptions about your future income in the short, intermediate, and long term.

After reviewing all your future income possibilities, an advisor can pick the best investment and withdrawal options to maximize your income while minimizing the taxes you'll pay in each money bucket, as I summarized in the last chapter.

When taxes are managed correctly, it's a powerful wealth builder. So, let's review some examples of how this works.

How Taxes Change With Each Money Bucket

The taxes you'll pay after retiring vary greatly, depending on whether you access your short-term, intermediate, or long-term money bucket.

To simply our discussion of taxes, here is a quick refresher on the four types of taxation:

1. Ordinary Income
2. Qualified Dividends and Capital Gains
3. Tax-Deferred Income
4. Tax-Free Income

Now, let's review how taxes can change with each money bucket.

Your first bucket is short-term cash.

Not surprisingly, this cash is taxed as ordinary income. For example, the interest earned on savings from a CD, money market, or savings account is subject to taxes. This is often overlooked.

As interest rates have risen in recent years to 5%, interest earnings have grown significantly. However, the interest is taxed at ordinary rates, thus lowering "real" earnings to 3.9% (assuming a 22% tax bracket).

You can see how these tax rates change based on your income in the table below. Note there are two columns, ordinary and capital gains taxes!

2024 Ordinary & Long-Term Capital Gains Tax Rates: Individual and Married Filing Jointly

Individual				Married Filing Jointly		
Income Up To...	Ordinary Income Tax Rate	Capital Gains Tax Rate		Income Up To...	Ordinary Income Tax Rate	Capital Gains Tax Rate
$11,600	10%	0% (to $47,025)		$23,200	10%	0% (to $94,050)
$47,150	12%			$94,300	12%	
$100,525	22%	15%		$201,050	22%	15%
$191,950	24%			$383,900	24%	
$243,725	32%			$487,450	32%	
$518,900	35%	20%		$583,750	35%	20%
$609,350				$731,200		
$609,350+	37%			$731,200+	37%	

www.clippingchains.com

The intermediate bucket holds your after-tax investments

Withdrawals from this bucket are taxed as capital gains and qualified dividends. This is where you have to be careful. While you don't want to be too heavy on withdrawals from this bucket, you have some leeway.

For example, you can have up to $80,000 of taxable income annually and not pay <u>any</u> taxes on qualified dividend withdrawals.

As for cashing out stocks, you will be taxed at capital gains rates. This means the most you'll ever pay is 20% of your gains. Losses can offset any gains, and the net is taxed at the capital gains rate. You can see capital gains tax rates in the chart above.

So, if you bought Apple at $100 per share and sold it at $200, you'll only pay capital gains (capped at 20%) even though you may be in an even higher tax bracket. This information is vital to know, yet many tax accountants won't talk with you about this because investments aren't their specialty, and most don't understand it!

Your last bucket is long-term retirement money.

This money is tax-deferred, meaning you will only pay taxes on withdrawals. However, if you plan ahead, some money here will be tax-free. So, let's take a quick trip back in time to see how this can happen.

Somewhere years ago, you started a 401K. Chances are, some employers matched your contributions to a certain level. Plus, you got tax deductions because your contributions were pre-tax. Not a bad deal!

As your career went on, you continued your contributions. Maybe you increased them as your income grew. Now, at the end of your career, you have a large IRA or 401K.

But someday, you will have to take money out of this bucket. In fact, the Feds will mandate that you do. And you will pay taxes on every withdrawal. This is called Required Minimum Distribution, or RMD. Fortunately, a strategy, Roth Conversions, can lower your taxes.

The Power of Roth Conversions

So, let's say you are now 62 and have a million dollars between your 401K and IRA investments. You're in a position where you don't need that money yet, and you have not elected to take your Social Security benefits. Perhaps you have other income, lower expenses, short-term investments that you can cash out, assets in your intermediate bucket, or all four.

So, you leave your money in your 401K/IRA long-term investments. Chances are, your million dollars will turn into 1.5 million by the time you're 70.

As of writing this book, you will have to take 4% of this money at age 70.5, thanks to Uncle Sam's RMD. You'll have no choice, whether you need the money or not. So, you withdraw $60K, and it's all taxable.

Keep in mind that the required minimum distribution increases as you age, as shown in the table below.

Uniform Lifetime Table					
Attained age	Distribution Period	Attained age	Distribution Period	Attained age	Distribution Period
72	27.4	89	12.9	105	4.6
73	26.5	90	12.2	106	4.3
74	25.5	91	11.5	107	4.1
75	24.6	92	10.8	108	3.9
76	23.7	93	10.1	109	3.7
77	22.9	94	9.5	110	3.5
78	22.0	95	8.9	111	3.4
79	21.1	96	8.4	112	3.3
80	20.2	97	7.8	113	3.1
81	19.4	98	7.3	114	3.0
82	18.5	99	6.8	115	2.9
83	17.7	100	6.4	116	2.8
84	16.8	101	6.0	117	2.7
85	16.0	102	5.6	118	2.5
86	15.2	103	5.2	119	2.3
87	14.4	104	4.9	120+	2.0
88	13.7				

On top of this, you also start collecting Social Security benefits if you haven't already done so. This is also partially taxable. How Social Security impacts your taxes depends, in part, on when you elect to take your benefit. Let's review this before we get back to Roth Conversions.

When should you take your Social Security Benefit?

Choosing the optimal time to elect your Social Security benefit is crucial and hinges on several key considerations. The primary factor is your age. While you can claim benefits as early as age 62, doing so results in a permanently reduced monthly payment.

Full retirement age (FRA) varies based on birth year but typically falls between 66 and 67. Electing to receive social security at FRA ensures you get 100% of your calculated benefit. Waiting until age 70 can increase your monthly benefit by up to 8% per year past FRA, maximizing your payout.

Whether you wait until age 70 to collect Social Security depends on your health and life expectancy, your financial needs, and whether you plan to continue working. If you are in good health and your family is long-lived, delaying benefits might be advantageous. On the other hand, claiming benefits earlier might be more practical if you need income sooner or have health concerns.

Another reason to wait until age 70 for Social Security may be whether your spouse is collecting benefits. Finally, you have to consider any tax implications.

As the graph below shows, your tax bracket can increase as you age, thanks to required minimum distributions and social security. This is why you can pay more taxes after age 70 than 65.

Tax Brackets During Retirement Can Be Surprising

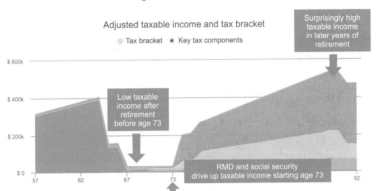

Fortunately, strategies can help decrease your tax bracket, with the Roth Conversion being the most common. Advisors often call this smoothing out your tax liability. Here's how it works.

How Roth Conversions Help You Save Money To Create More Wealth

A Roth Conversion strategy involves moving assets from a traditional retirement account, such as an IRA or 401(k), to a Roth IRA. The converted amount is taxed as ordinary income, but Roth IRA withdrawals are tax-free if they meet certain conditions. This can offer several benefits, including:

Tax savings

A Roth conversion can help reduce your overall tax bill if you expect a higher income during retirement. This can be especially beneficial if you convert assets when you're in a relatively lower tax bracket.

No required minimum distributions

Roth IRAs don't have required minimum distributions as traditional IRAs do, starting at age 73.

Investment gains

Withdrawals from a Roth IRA are tax-free if the account has been held for at least five years or if the account holder is at least 59.5 years old. This can lead to significant investment gains that won't be taxed over the account's life.

Now that I've summarized the benefits of a Roth Conversion, let's rewind our story to age 65 when you were in a lower tax bracket. In the first version of our story, you left your money in 401K and IRA long-term investments. However, this time, you followed a different strategy.

This time, you withdrew money from your IRA or 401K in your sixties. You paid taxes on it, but you paid less taxes because you were in a lower tax bracket. Then, you converted your withdrawal to a Roth, which is not subject to a required minimum distribution. So this money can sit in the Roth as long as you like, and you - or your heirs - will never pay taxes on it again.

The graph below shows how this works and the significant benefit you gain from a Roth Conversion.

Smoothing Out The Tax Liability

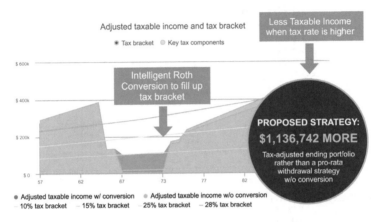

Adjusted taxable income and tax bracket

● Tax bracket   ○ Key tax components

Less Taxable Income when tax rate is higher

Intelligent Roth Conversion to fill up tax bracket

PROPOSED STRATEGY:

$1,136,742 MORE

Tax-adjusted ending portfolio rather than a pro-rata withdrawal strategy w/o conversion

● Adjusted taxable income w/ conversion   ● Adjusted taxable income w/o conversion
— 10% tax bracket   — 15% tax bracket   — 25% tax bracket   — 28% tax bracket

This is why a Roth is a fantastic wealth distribution vehicle, too. Whether it's a Roth conversion or a Roth IRA, this is the ideal asset to leave for your kids. Why? Because it will be tax-free for them, too.

This is how saving on taxes creates more wealth down the road. And, like most financial advisors, I use software that illustrates different options with Roth conversions. That way, you can see how much money you'll save in taxes and the extra wealth you'll create because of it.

Here is an example of a well-thought-out Roth Conversion Strategy, which schedules IRA withdrawals in low-income years before the required minimum withdrawals at age 73.

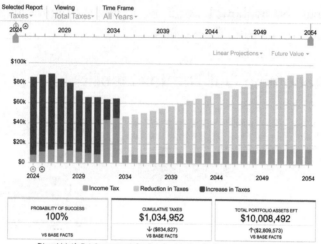

This graph is just for illustration purposes only. Consult your financial and tax advisor for your own personal information.

As you've seen in this chapter, saving on taxes is a crucial way to create more long-term wealth, but it isn't the only way. In the next chapter, we'll cover two more methods.

If you want to see how Roth Conversions can affect your tax bracket and potentially save lifetime taxation, contact us at 440-617-9100 or through www.eliosfinancial.com to arrange a meeting, either online or in my office. We will run a complimentary analysis to determine the best course of action for your investments.

CHAPTER 07

TWO MORE KEYS TO LONG-TERM WEALTH: DIVERSIFICATION AND LOW FEES

"Diversification works over the long term. You get rich by concentration… but you stay rich by diversification."
– Warren Buffett

Warren Buffett had a point.

While concentrating your investments can potentially lead to wealth creation, it's crucial to maintain that wealth over the long term through diversification. In other words, you might "get rich" by focusing on a few key investments, but to "stay rich" and preserve your wealth, you should diversify your portfolio to manage risk effectively.

You will see tremendous gains if you can get in early on a rising stock, like Nvidia recently or Amazon, Google, and Microsoft years ago. But knowing what individual stocks to invest in can be like searching for a needle in the haystack - unless you have legendary stock picker Warren Buffett advising you.

Diversification reduces volatility and potential risk. If planned right, investments in your portfolio can offset losses when investments in other sectors are doing poorly. Plus, a well-planned, diversified portfolio will continue to grow, so you can keep sleeping at night.

How Diversification Keeps You Rich

Diversification can be applied in many different ways. However, the most important thing is to get the right mix of stocks, bonds, alternative investments, and cash. In other words, what you diversify are the different asset classes in your portfolio.

Asset classes—such as stocks, bonds, and cash—usually behave differently under similar market and economic conditions. Keep in mind that these asset classes have sub-asset classes, too.

For example, sub-classes of stocks include large, small, and mid-cap stocks. You also have growth or value stocks and even stocks that blend these two sub-assets, not to mention domestic and international stocks.

You can also invest in different types of bonds. As for alternative investment assets, you have opportunities in real estate, commodities, cryptocurrency, and precious metals. This class includes REITs and MLPs as well.

The chart below illustrates different asset classes, including a diversified portfolio, shown by the black line. Over the long run, a diversified portfolio outperforms all classes except U.S. small-cap stocks. It also has less volatility, which can give you peace of mind.

A financial advisor considers the overall potential risk and return and how different asset classes correlate with one another to help you determine the right asset allocation for your portfolio.

For example, right now, people are excited about getting a guaranteed 5% on their cash. That may work in the near future, but not over the long term. Rates will come down eventually, and after taxes and inflation, it will not be enough to build long-term wealth. So, having the right mix in the right proportions is important.

Equally important is the need to regularly manage your portfolio to ensure that your asset classes reflect the best options for your

---

11 https://www.schwab.com/learn/story/why-diversification-matters

time horizon and goals. While you can't control markets, you can control the risk and the balance of your investments.

Asset Allocation is Your Friend

Investors choose the types and proportions of stocks, bonds, and other securities in a portfolio through asset allocation. A well-designed portfolio with a good asset allocation can help produce more consistent returns through diversification.

In 1986, a study by Gary Brinson, Gilbert Beebower, and Randolph Hood analyzed returns for different time periods. They discovered that asset allocation accounted for 93.6% of the studied portfolio's quarterly returns variation. During a follow-up study in 1991, they concluded that 91% of portfolio returns are determined by asset allocation.[12] Put in another way, it's the asset classes and the mix that determines your overall outcome- even more than the specific stocks, bonds, mutual funds or ETFs you own.

The balance of the returns can be attributed to other factors, such as security selection and market timing. I have always believed in the right mix of stocks, bonds, and cash. This diversification has served many investors well over a long investment period.

What Is the Efficient Frontier?

The efficient frontier is the set of optimal portfolios that offer the highest expected return for a defined level of risk or the lowest

---

[12] Tokat, Yesim. The Asset Allocation Debate: Provocative Questions, Enduring Realities APRIL 2005. Apr. 2005.

risk for a given level of expected return. Portfolios that lie below the efficient frontier are sub-optimal because they do not provide enough return for the level of risk. Portfolios that cluster to the right of the efficient frontier are sub-optimal because they have a higher level of risk for the defined rate of return.

The graph below shows The Efficient Frontier and how the right mix of stocks, bonds, and cash will determine over 91% of your returns.

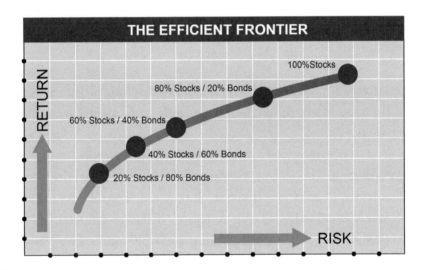

To grow and protect your retirement fund, it's not just about owning Nvidia or Apple stock. It is about being in the right mix of stocks, bonds and cash- your asset allocation.

Finally, never try to time the market. Chances are, you already know this, but it is so important that it bears repeating here. Diversifying among asset classes is the key to growing and protecting your money. Always remember: Time in the market, not timing the market!

In summary, diversification is a critical way to reduce risk and grow money, but it's not the only way.

Why Lower Fees Mean Bigger Returns On Your Money

All else being equal, lower fees win when it comes to getting bigger returns. Fortunately, we can control fees. So, knowing what your investments cost can save you a lot of money.

Yet surprisingly, a recent survey found that more than a fifth of investors don't think they pay any fees for their investment accounts.

According to the survey conducted by the Financial Industry Regulatory Authority Investor Education Foundation, 21% of investors said they don't pay fees to invest in non-retirement accounts when, in actuality, they probably do.[13] Even more surprising, an additional 17% of investors said they didn't know how much they paid in fees. This knowledge gap could cost these investors big money in the long term.

---

[13] Lin, Judy, et al. *Investors in the United States: The Changing Landscape a Report of the FINRA Foundation National Financial Capability Study Authors: Acknowledgements.* 2022.

Investors have been surprised by the following fees

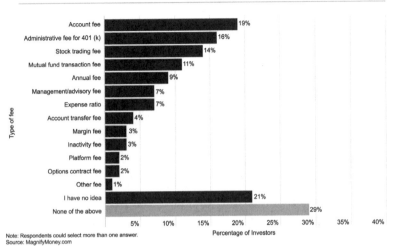

Note: Respondents could select more than one answer.
Source: MagnifyMoney.com

For example, a typical fee for all mutual funds is the expense ratio, which is charged annually. This ratio is the fund management cost, given as a percentage. Since this annual fee is based on the amount of money you have invested in the fund, the more you invest, the more you pay.

Typically, this fee is paid out of fund assets, so you'll never see an invoice. But rest assured, it will come out of your returns. That means if your mutual fund returns 7.5% but has an expense ratio of 1.5%, you only earn 6.0% on your shares.

In addition to the expense ratio, some funds include other costs, like purchase and redemption fees. These fees are a percentage of the value of the shares you're buying or selling. Plus, you'll likely pay other annual expenses, too.

Now, mutual funds aren't the only place where you pay fees. You also pay sales charges, also known as loads and commissions, with most brokerage firms. You might pay a front-end load when you buy shares or a back-end load when selling. As for commissions, you pay these fees to the broker for their services.

And there are even more fees that I haven't mentioned here.

The Problems With Fees

We have a problem in the financial industry. It's called lack of transparency.

Fees are often presented in a way that makes them appear low - or in some cases - they're wrapped up in jargon on the third page of a long-winded agreement that you scan over before signing. This is why fees are a hidden cost for most investors.

One of the worst offenders of hidden fees is annuities. Variable annuities are costly, yet most investors are unaware of the fees because they are buried in a 50-page prospectus.

For visible fees, many investors ignore them because an amount like 2% seems deceptively low. Unfortunately, when a fee is given as a percentage, it doesn't reveal how much you'll pay for lost returns.

So, how much of a difference does it make? Consider these two scenarios:

Scenario 1

Suppose you invested $80,000 for 25 years. You earned 7% per year and paid 0.50% in annual fees. At the end of the 25 years, you made approximately $380,000.

Scenario 2

This time, you invested the same amount but paid 2.0% annually. After 25 years, you're left with approximately $260,000. That "small" 2.0% cost you $120,000.[14]

This is why I work carefully with new clients to examine the fee structure of every investment they have. If I can find equal investments for lower costs, you can bet we'll make the switch wherever possible.

The Power of Indexing and Exchange-Traded Funds

I often choose low-cost indexing and exchange-traded funds (ETFs) over mutual funds. These funds offer lower fees, which results in better long-term returns. Plus, they are one of the easiest ways to diversify your portfolio. To quote another investment legend, John C. Bogle, who founded Vanguard, "Don't look for the needle in the haystack. Just buy the haystack!"

Many successful investors have indeed followed John Bogle's advice and harnessed the power of index investing. Index funds involve

---

[14] https://www.investopedia.com/investing/costs-investing/

passive investing, using a long-term strategy without actively picking securities or timing the market. Index funds match the risk and return of the market based on the theory that, in the long term, the market will outperform any single investment.

Overall, diversification and lower fees give you better results. Both are essential ways to mitigate risk. In Chapter 10, I'll summarize the different ways to lower your financial risk so you can get the best possible results, but in the next chapter, we'll look at a more personal way to ensure you have a long, happy retirement.

If you would like to examine and analyze your investment fees, contact us at https://www.eliosfinancial.com/ to book a complimentary meeting. We'll review your assets and provide a summary report on where you can lower fees and save money.

CHAPTER 08

WEALTH THAT IS TRULY PRICELESS: YOUR GOOD HEALTH

"Health is a priceless wealth. Invest while you can."
– Bryant McGill

There's one axiom I remind myself of nearly every day: All the money in the world won't matter if you're not alive to enjoy it.

Of course, ultimately, we have no control over when it's our time to leave. But there are some things we *can* control when it comes to increasing our chances of living a longer life.

As the quote above says, you can invest in your health now to increase your chances of enjoying a long, fulfilling retirement. To put it another way, if you accumulate money at the expense of your health, then you may end up using this money to pay for your health in later years.

Like so many things, juggling health and wealth is a balancing act. You need to make money and save it for your future peace of mind. After all, a retirement free of money worries positively influences your physical and mental health.

However, don't make the mistake of sacrificing your health to make money. Preparing yourself physically to enjoy your retirement is just as important as saving money for it. You'll see why in the next section.

Proof That Good Health Can Help You Enjoy Retirement

You've probably heard that regular exercise is linked to a decreased risk of health problems like heart disease, high blood pressure, diabetes, and cancer. These health problems not only make your life difficult and uncomfortable, but they also bring significant expenses in medical fees, doctor's visits, medication, and more.

Without a doubt, exercise helps you live longer. But by how much?

A recent study in the American Heart Association journal Circulation has shown the amount of exercise needed to reduce one's risk of death. More than 116,000 adults completed questionnaires on their activity levels for 30 years. Researchers then compared the time these adults spent on activity and exercise with their death rates.

People who spent 300 to 600 minutes per week in moderate physical activity had a 28% to 38% lower mortality rate for *any* cause of death, whether it was cardiovascular disease, illness, or an accident.

Just as interesting, earlier studies had already shown that participating in moderate physical activities for 150 to 299 minutes per week lowered all-cause mortality rates by 19% to 25%.[15]

So, let's put this into perspective.

If you spend 2.5 hours a week in moderate physical activity, you reduce your risk of dying from any cause by 19%. If you can increase that to 10 hours per week, you reduce this risk by 38%.

So, what do they mean by moderate physical activity? According to the Harvard T.H. Chan School of Public Health, this includes a brisk walk, mowing your lawn, vacuuming, washing windows, bicycling with light effort, or playing tennis doubles.[16]

And if you're into more vigorous activities, like jogging, soccer, or shoveling snow, you can reduce your mortality by a similar amount in less time.

But reducing mortality isn't the only benefit you'll get from exercise.

---

[15] https://www.ahajournals.org/doi/10.1161/CIRCULATIONAHA.121.058162?cookie Set=1

[16] https://www.hsph.harvard.edu/obesity-prevention-source/moderate-and-vigorous-physical-activity/

Why I Do Everything I Can To Encourage Good Health

Years ago, my mother-in-law was diagnosed with ovarian cancer that had metastasized to her lung. Her excellent care and treatment at the Cleveland Clinic improved her quality of life, but after a long battle, she succumbed to the disease in 2020.

While I couldn't control how she suffered near the end of her life, I could do something else. I decided to raise money by participating in The Cleveland Clinic's annual VeloSano fundraiser (www.velosano.org).

This 12-mile, 25-mile, 50-mile, and 100-mile weekend bike ride raises money for cancer research and therapies at the Cleveland Clinic. I decided to do my part in raising money to help others.

However, this story doesn't end here.

In my second year of participating in the fundraiser, I met Mat G., who shared many interests with me. We became really great friends, riding together and sharing a room during the two-day, 200-mile weekend ride.

Naturally, I expected to be his roommate again for our year three ride. So when he told me he couldn't be my roommate, I thought he was kidding. That was, until he told me that his doctor didn't want him to participate because he had stage 3 colon cancer.

Here he was, tall, strong, and an incredible athlete. Yet, at the age of 51, he had cancer.

Mat fought a valiant fight and continued to raise money for cancer research. Tragically, he died of colorectal cancer 24 months later. Today, I continue our tradition of riding in his honor, too. I'm currently preparing for my 9th year of fundraising, and so far, I've raised more than $70,000 for cancer research over the last 10 years.

Just as important, I have learned that health isn't something I can take for granted. This is why I am doing everything in my power to stay healthy and vibrant for as long as I can. While I can't control whether I will get an illness or experience an accident, I will know that I did everything I could to live a full and healthy life as possible for myself and my family.

Exercise Improves Your Memory and Mental Health

Harvard Medical School reports that exercise helps memory in several ways. Exercise has been shown to reduce insulin resistance and inflammation while also stimulating the release of growth factors. Growth factors are chemicals that help your brain grow new blood vessels and brain cells.

A recent study saw the benefit of these growth factors. Researchers found that people who started a simple exercise program increased their brain volumes, especially in the areas that control thinking and memory.

The study participants hadn't exercised regularly before. Yet they saw improvement in just six months to a year of walking briskly, for one hour, twice a week. Put another way, they increased their brain volume with two hours of moderate physical activity every week.[17]

On top of this, the researchers also found that this exercise improved mood and sleep while reducing stress and anxiety.

Not bad, right?

So, if you're not exercising now, I encourage you to get started. If you need a little guidance and motivation, I have something to recommend.

Guidance To Get You Going

When it comes to anti-aging and wellness, one of my favorite motivational books is "Younger Next Year: Live Strong, Fit, and

---

[17] https://www.health.harvard.edu/blog/regular-exercise-changes-brain-improve-memory-thinking-skills-201404097110

Sexy—Until You're 80 and Beyond." I have recommended this book many times over the years.

The book was written by a retired lawyer, Chris Crowley, and Henry S. Lodge, M.D., in 2007. It was a runaway hit then and is still highly relevant today. There are now several books in this series, all dedicated to helping people live active, pain-free lives.

If this interests you even a little, you can go here for more information: https://www.youngernextyear.com/

How A Solid Retirement Plan Helps When The Unexpected Happens

Life can certainly take a turn when you least expect it. This can happen no matter how well you take care of yourself.

I recently had two clients who were both married, in their early to mid-60s, and getting ready for retirement. Each client had a solid plan and ample financial resources to carry them through a long, comfortable retirement.

Yet, in both cases, their spouse was diagnosed with cancer. Suddenly, the perspective changed. Now, instead of spending their "Go-Go" years of retirement, traveling, enjoying hobbies and grandkids, they are facing what might be a lifelong battle. Unfortunately, one spouse had a stage four diagnosis and had only another year or two to live.

However, there is a silver lining to these tragic stories. We revised each couple's plan to ensure money was available for their new health needs. This was so much better than having no plan and no idea if they had the resources they needed.

So, while you can't control everything that happens with your health, a good retirement plan will help you or your loved ones if needed.

Now, let's move on to your final step: choosing the right financial advisor to help you achieve your retirement goals.

> To book a complimentary consultation with me, whether online or in person, contact us at https://www.eliosfinancial.com/ to arrange a time that is convenient for you.

CHAPTER 09

HOW TO MOVE YOUR RETIREMENT FORWARD WITH A FINANCIAL ADVISOR

"Often, when you think you're at the end of something, you're at the beginning of something else."

– Fred Rogers

This is an exciting time. Your retirement may be just a few years ahead. Or maybe you're very close to exiting. Either way, it's time to start planning your descent down the mountain.

Which Path Do You Take Now?

You have three choices:

Do Nothing

You can keep your accounts where they are now, staying with the same investment firm, broker, or workplace provider.

However, by now, you may have realized there could be holes in your retirement planning. And there are likely other issues that you need to consider.

If you've come this far, I'm betting you aren't going to do "nothing." You are likely going to take action. The question is...what?

Do-It-Yourself

You could use the information you've learned to do more research, or you could go to your financial planner and ask more questions. Both options will likely put you in a better position to plan your retirement.

But if you aren't satisfied with the answers you get, or you would rather not do it on your own, it may be time to talk with a financial advisor. And there are so many reasons why you shouldn't do this on your own.

For instance, I recently met with a couple who had already retired. I'll call them Fred and Carol. Fred's successful career in engineering allowed him to accumulate a seven-figure portfolio. He did this without help, managing his own investments. With this couple, Carol knew very little about the money and how it was managed. She trusted Fred. He handled everything, and she was fine with this.

But, not long ago, Carol noticed that Fred would forget where he put his car keys and other little things. Over time, little things turned into bigger things. They knew something wasn't right.

Finally, after seeing doctors, Fred was diagnosed with early-onset Alzheimer's disease.

They both knew the day was approaching when Fred would no longer be able to manage the money. And they also knew that Carol was not prepared or willing to fill in for Fred.

This is when they met with me.

Fred and Carol's situation is a reminder that anything can happen at any time. Hopefully, you will never face Fred's situation. However, wouldn't it be prudent to meet with a financial advisor before anything happens?

You can get to know him or her, ask questions, share ideas, and see if this person is someone you might want to work with, whether your situation is urgent—like Fred and Carol's—or not.

And if you're wondering about the expense of working with an advisor, it may be more important to consider the value an advisor provides.

The Value Provided By Financial Advisors

First, it's important to note the difference between a financial planner/advisor and an investment advisor. While both offer similar services, financial advisors and planners assist with a wider range of topics. Advisors can help you develop a plan that covers investment management, income and expense planning, taxes, as well as retirement and estate planning.

By providing these extra services, advisors deliver value at a level roughly triple the typical advisory fee of 1%, or about 3%. In other words, the long-term value far exceeds the fee.

This was the conclusion of the Vanguard Advisor Research Study 2010 - 2022. The study arrived at the 3% figure by calculating the additional returns an advisor generates across five categories. Here's how they broke it down:

1. Using cost-effective strategies such as lowering fees: 45 basis points
2. Rebalancing your portfolio when changes are needed: 35 basis points
3. Correcting behavioral mistakes such as recency bias: 1.50 basis points
4. Locating assets in correct accounts and stocks: 0 to 75 basis points
5. Developing a strategy to withdraw your funds: 0 to 70 points

A study by Russell Investments Canada Ltd. also resulted in a similar value. They found the value of an advisor who performs comprehensive wealth management to be 2.88% in 2020.[18]

So, it's clear that a financial advisor provides value. However, choosing an advisor who works best for you is also important.

---

[18] https://www.advisor.ca/practice/planning-and-advice/advisors-add-2-88-in-value-study-finds/

What does an RIA (Registered Investment Advisor) Charge?

Registered Investment Advisors (RIAs) charge clients annual fees as a percentage of the assets they manage, typically between 1% and 2%. The average RIA fee in 2019 was 1.17% of assets under management (AUM).

However, fees can range from 0.5% to 2% of AUM, depending on the services provided and the amount of assets managed. For example, an RIA might charge 1.5% for equities like stocks and 0.75% for fixed-income investments like bonds.

Fees are usually recalculated every three months to reflect changes in market value. For example, if the market declines, the fee will also decline. Clients with more assets can usually negotiate lower fees, sometimes as low as 0.50%. This aligns the client's interests with the RIA's, as the advisor can't make more money on the account unless the client's assets increase.

The alignment of fees and assets under management as a fiduciary duty is crucial because it ensures that clients receive advice that is unbiased and aligned with their financial goals and needs. It helps build trust between clients and their advisors, knowing that their advisor is committed to acting in their best interests at all times.

How Do You Choose The Right Financial Advisor?

Like any professional, not all advisors are created equal. So it pays to shop around.

You can start by asking other successful individuals in your network who they use. You can also ask people you work with. It can be helpful if the advisor has experience working with people from your company.

One of the most critical questions is whether an advisor has fiduciary responsibilities. But what is a Fiduciary?

The term "fiduciary advisor" is often used in the context of financial services and investment advice. According to the SEC (U.S. Securities and Exchange Commission), a fiduciary advisor is a financial professional who is legally obligated to act in the best interests of their clients. This means they must put their client's interests ahead of their own and provide advice that suits the client's best interests.

Fiduciary advisors are held to a higher standard of conduct than non-fiduciary advisors. They are required to provide full disclosure of any potential conflicts of interest and avoid engaging in transactions that could compromise their clients' interests. Additionally, fiduciary advisors are required to adhere to specific regulations and standards set by regulatory bodies like the SEC.

In summary, working with a fiduciary is important because:

- Fiduciaries are licensed by the US Securities and Exchange Commission (SEC).
- They are required to represent the client's best interest.
- They must offer sound, objective advice.
- They have expertise in financial planning, retirement, taxes, investment management, and more.
- Plus, they do not charge commissions but instead use transparent, flat-fee pricing.

Fiduciaries are required by law to be unbiased and put the interests of their clients first. They must disclose any potential conflicts of interest. Their compensation is not influenced by commissions or sales. Overall, a fiduciary relationship is built on loyalty, honesty, transparency, and, most importantly, TRUST.

Does Your Advisor Blend The Latest Technology With His Or Her Expertise?

This is another crucial question to ask. Your advisor should be comfortable using technology in addition to his or her advice and experience. Always remember: The person using the tool is far more important than the tool itself.

At the risk of being obsolete or dated in the near future, here's a quick list from Investopedia of software used by forward-thinking advisors.

- Comprehensive financial planning software for cash flow analysis, long-term planning, and tax strategy plans

- Portfolio management software to provide comprehensive performance reporting of your assets and holdings
- Daily feed trading/rebalancing software that automates and coordinates your portfolio trans-actions
- Account Aggregation software that enables a daily fee and connection to all financial accounts in one dashboard
- Investment analytics software that provides all-encompassing data and historical information regarding securities and other investments
- Risk tolerance software that identifies, navigates, and quantifies hidden and known portfolio risks
- Document management software that makes it easy to send you documents and get your signature[19]

Today, most of this software is powered by AI. It is designed to make planning faster and easier while still allowing an advisor to provide a critical human perspective.

In addition to determining whether an advisor has fiduciary responsibilities, there are other questions you should consider:

- What is their fee structure?
- Is the advisor located in your area and accessible for meeting in person? Or do they meet virtually as well?

---

[19] https://www.investopedia.com/articles/professionals/080615/top-5-software-pro-grams-used-financial-advisors.asp

- What are the advisor's qualifications? This question lets you talk about their background and why they became a financial advisor.
- What services do they offer? Be sure to let them know if you have special needs, such as paying off debt or saving for college.
- What is their investment philosophy? Does it match yours?
- How often do they get in touch with clients, and by what means? Do they use email? Phone calls? What about personal meetings?

By asking these questions, you can determine whether an advisor is a good fit for you and your family. After all, you will likely spend years together. They will be a partner in ensuring your retirement is everything you want it to be. Choose wisely.

If you want to meet with me to see how I can help you meet your retirement goals, contact us at https://www.eliosfinancial.com to arrange an online or in-person meeting. I can answer any questions you may have, and there is no obligation.

CHAPTER 10

YOUR SUMMARY ON MANAGING FINANCIAL RISK SO YOU CAN ENJOY YOUR RETIREMENT

"Money grows on the tree of persistence."

– Japanese proverb

Throughout this book, you've seen that it takes not one but several steps to mitigate risk and enjoy higher returns on your investments. Remember, anything that can lower your returns, such as high fees, is considered a risk factor.

These steps are so essential that I'm summarizing them here for a quick and handy reference.

Be Aware Of Your Mindset

Always remember, as human beings, we are subject to all types of emotions, biases, and behaviors. Any one of these factors can influence our decision-making, especially when it comes to finances.

So before you make any financial decisions, especially a major one, talk with a trusted financial advisor.

I've had many examples of clients needing perspective for their financial decisions. Most have been around buying stocks at all-time highs, selling stocks at all-time lows, or making large withdrawals from deferred accounts, causing significant tax liability. But this isn't the only example of why you may need to seek advice from your advisor when it comes to mindset.

Recently, a client I had worked with for over 15 years was laid off from his banking job. He was 60 years old at the time and had planned on working to age 65. Unfortunately, it was no longer his choice. However, he was not ready psychologically to retire. But after carefully reviewing his entire financial picture, he felt he could bridge the gap to Social Security and make the cash flow work fine. The relief he felt was palpable. His mindset had changed entirely. This is how a good advisor can help when it comes to your peace of mind.

Talking with your advisor will help you step back and look at every angle of a situation before you take action. That way, you can decide based on all factors instead of an emotional or biased reaction. This step is one of the most critical yet easiest ways to mitigate risk. But it's not the only one.

Don't Make Short- Term Decisions On Long- Term Money or Long- Term Decisions On Short- Term Money

This axiom is closely related to your mindset. If you have a fearful mindset and you're not working with a financial advisor, you can easily make irrational decisions, which increases your risk of losing money.

A study completed by the independent financial evaluator, DALBAR, Inc., found that the average investor underperformed the S&P 500 by 4.66% per year between 2006 and 2015. They concluded this poor performance was caused primarily by investors selling stocks when markets were down and then missing out on the market rebounds that followed.[20]

This is an example of making short-term decisions about what should be long-term money in the stock market. And you can bet these decisions are tied to fear and emotional decision-making. This is why the next risk-reducing step is also important.

Focus On What You Can Control

No one can control the markets, elections, wars, and other events. This is why you should never consider these factors in financial planning. Fortunately, there are five factors you *can* control, which should be considered and then included in your retirement plan.

---

[20] https://cowrywise.com/blog/behavioural-finance/ AND https://cdn2.hubspot.net/hubfs/5341408/EP_Wealth_Advisors_April2019/pdf/2016-Dalbar-QAIB-Report.pdf

Spending:

While traditional planners recommend that you include a spending strategy for each of the three stages of retirement: Go-Go, Slow-Go, and No-Go, I like to plan for Go-Go throughout your retirement. This way, you can be more confident that you can enjoy things you've always wanted to do while staying within your budget.

Savings:

You've saved money for years to ensure that you will have money for retirement. So, it's critical to protect this money as much as possible while also allowing it to grow. You can do this by managing your three money buckets:

Short Term: Liquid Assets

This is the money you will need in the next 12 months. The goal is to keep it liquid and safe, in cash or vehicles like money market funds.

Intermediate: Invested Money

Your intermediate savings is your taxable investment portfolio. Here, you should diversify your investments so your money can grow safely.

Long-term: Retirement Money

This is your retirement nest egg. Most people have this money in qualified retirement vehicles like 401Ks or 403Bs, annuities, and IRAs.

Remember, you need to manage each money bucket differently depending on your time horizon, goals, income needs, and more.

Timing:
Timing is when you decide events such as when you'll retire, take Social Security, or make withdrawals. The goal is to reduce the taxes you'll pay so you can keep more of your money.

Risk:
Almost everything I've covered in this book deals with risk. The good news is that you can take steps to control risk based on where you're at now. By working with a financial advisor, you can create a plan to lower your risk while maximizing opportunities for higher returns.

Legacy:
If you want to leave money for your heirs, charities, or both, you can take steps now to reduce estate fees and probate costs.

Summary:
Working with your financial advisor to manage these five factors will help you focus on what you can control. However, you can take five additional steps to reduce risk further. Let's drill down on these steps now, starting with taxes.

Mitigate Your Taxes

Always remember: It's not only the amount you make in returns that matters—it's how much you keep after taxes. Even losing small amounts of money to taxes adds up over time and reduces your long-term wealth.

Unfortunately, while many investors understand markets and investments, figuring out taxes is a whole other ball game. This is where working with a well-aligned advisor is critical.

The good news is that with planning, you can make your portfolio more tax-efficient and keep a greater share of your hard-earned money.

The next step will not only help you keep more of your money, it can also help your money grow.

Diversify Your Portfolio

Diversification is one of the best ways to reduce risk in your portfolio while capturing gains and building wealth.

Between 1926 and 2019, a portfolio consisting entirely of stocks returned 10.3% on average. This was the highest across all asset classes. However, this return also came with extreme volatility. At worst, stocks lost 43% in one year, and at best, they hit a high of 54%.[21]

That's quite a roller coaster ride! If you can keep emotions out of the picture and your money in for the long haul, this will build more wealth for you. However, when you're retired, exposing yourself to this risk is not the way to go.

On the other hand, the traditional 60/40 portfolio saw an average annual historical return of 8.8% in the same period, with a lot less

---

[21] https://www.visualcapitalist.com/90-years-stock-and-bond-portfolio-performance/

volatility. Or, if you had your money in a 100% bond portfolio, you would have earned 5.3%. That's even less volatility, but it also means much lower returns than the traditional 60/40 portfolio.

You can probably see why Warren Buffett says diversification is the best way to *preserve* wealth. But there is yet another way to ensure greater returns.

Pay Lower Fees

Every investment you own costs money. Unfortunately, these costs are often buried in the fine print of a lengthy agreement. Or they're stated in a way where the actual cost to the investor isn't clear. As a result, many investors have no clue about the fees they're paying.

For example, you might see an expense ratio of 2% in their mutual fund and brush it off as small and nothing to worry about. But, as we saw earlier, this means instead of getting the 7% your mutual fund made this year, you'll see 5% after your fee. That's a lot of money over many years.

The bottom line is that paying lower fees means more significant returns. Period. This is why you can save money by having your financial advisor sort through your investments to ensure you pay the lowest fees possible. If you're not, it may be time to switch investments.

Your final two risk-reducing steps make implementing all the steps I mentioned above easier.

Develop A Retirement Plan

If you don't have a retirement plan yet, you may have many reasons why.

For one, life is busy. With so many competing priorities, it can be difficult to stop, sit down with a financial advisor, and work on a plan.

You may have planned to rely on the company that holds your investments, such as Fidelity, or you may even be planning to take care of your retirement plan yourself.

Whatever your reason may be, it can only help to meet with a financial advisor. You can ask questions. Share your ideas. See what he or she has to say and how they can help. You may be surprised at what you learn.

And finally, there is one more important way to mitigate your risk.

Keep Track of the Retirement Plan You Have

Once you have a plan, be sure to meet with your advisor regularly. Over time, you will need to rebalance your portfolio to keep your asset allocations on track. This will involve selling and buying assets, which means you will also need to consider taxes.

Working with an advisor who does this regularly will make your life easier and ensure you get the best returns with the least risk.

And that's what you deserve for your retirement.

I would be happy to provide a complimentary review of your current retirement plan or an assessment of your options if you don't have a plan at this point.

Simply contact us at https://www.eliosfinancial.com to arrange a meeting, either online or in person.

CONCLUSION

"You are never too old to set another goal or to dream a new dream."

– C. S. Lewis

I opened this book with a quote, and now I'm closing with one. I feel this quote is appropriate. After all, one of the best things about retirement is having the freedom to try new things and follow the road where it takes you.

You now have a blueprint for developing a solid retirement plan to help you do this.

A solid retirement plan should help you manage your money through asset allocation, risk reduction, insurance, debt management, tax reduction, and cash flow.

It should help you achieve your goals, whether you want to travel, relocate to your dream location, or re-create your life.

Your plan should give you peace of mind, knowing everything is organized and in control. You can sleep at night, no matter what happens in the markets. And you can rest assured that your loved ones will be taken care of when you are gone.

Perhaps the most fulfilling part of a solid retirement plan is knowing you can accomplish your life's purpose, not only in what you do but also in the legacy you leave behind.

Now, you just need to take the next step.

You can use this book as a guide to create a plan with your financial advisor or work with me and my team.

Whatever you decide, the most important thing is to get started now. The sooner you do, the more time you'll have to put your plan in place, so your assets can grow and your goals become reality.

And if you're already retired, it's never too late to revisit your goals and change strategies where needed. Even just a few tweaks in your retirement plan can mean a world of difference in how long your money will last and what you'll be able to achieve.

So get started. And here's to your long, fulfilling, and enlightened retirement!

Your Next Steps:

1. Visit us at www.EliosFinancial.com
2. Gather your information from the checklist at our website.
3. Answer a Confidential Questionnaire found on the website.
4. Call us to start a conversation!

www.EliosFinancial.com

ABOUT THE AUTHOR

James T. Elios, MBA, ChFC®, CLU®, AIF®

Jim is the founder of Elios Financial Group, an SEC-Registered Investment Advisor (RIA), and a Registered Principal of Private Client Services. As an independent financial advisor, Jim specializes in comprehensive financial planning and investment management.

Experience: He has more than 30 years of experience in the Financial Services industry, including retail banking with National City Bank, Cleveland, and as a financial planner with Cleveland Financial Group/Lincoln Financial Advisors. Jim is a frequent public speaker on financial planning issues, the economy, and financial markets. He has provided workshops for companies, government, non-profits, and charity organizations including the Social Security Administration. He has provided financial planning advice and guidance to many employees of local companies, such as Lincoln Electric, AT&T, Fairview Hospital/Cleveland Clinic, Sherwin Williams, and Progressive. He has contributed as a past columnist for the Plain Dealer's "Ask the Expert" feature column. Jim has made many local Cleveland media appearances including television on Action Channel 19 News and radio on The Lannigan Show 105.7 WMJI. He completed a due diligence trip to Asia, including Singapore, Hong Kong, and China, where he gave a lecture to students at Zhejiang University City College in Hangzhou, China.

Education: He graduated from Bowling Green State University with a Bachelor of Science in Business Administration (BSBA) with a concentration in marketing and finance. He obtained his Masters of Business Administration (MBA) in 1991 from Baldwin Wallace College. He has also obtained advanced financial designations, Chartered Financial Consultant (ChFC)® and Charter Life Underwriter (CLU) from The American College in Bryn Mawr, PA. He is also an Accredited Investment Fiduciary AIF) granted by ANSI National Accreditation Board (ANAB)®. He is securities registered through FINRA (www.finra.com) and holds Series 24, 7, and 63 registrations.

Personal: Jim resides in Avon Lake with his wife, Solveig, and their 3 children. He has lived in the area for over 40 years and is a graduate of North Olmsted High School. He enjoys biking, music, fitness and travel and most of all spending time with his family.

Made in the USA
Columbia, SC
03 February 2025

53258733R00065